For Chocolate Lovers

For Chocolate Lovers

FROM TRUFFLES TO TIRAMISU

THE TANNER BROTHERS

with photography by Peter Cassidy

jacqui
small

First published in 2006 by Jacqui Small,
an imprint of Aurum Press,
25 Bedford Avenue, London WC1B 3AT

Publisher Jacqui Small
Managing Editor Nicola Graimes
Art Director Ashley Western
Stylist Roisin Nield
Production Peter Colley

A catalogue record for this book is available from the British Library.

ISBN-10: 1 903221 62 5
ISBN-13: 978 1 903221 62 4

2008   2007   2006

10 9 8 7 6 5 4 3 2 1

Printed and bound in China

Page 1: Chocolate tiramisu
Page 2: Chocolate brownies

Contents

Chocolate is pure comfort food to us. From our first mouthful as children – we were always first in the queue to lick the spoon – to making decadent desserts in our restaurant and brasserie, chocolate is something we have always loved and enjoyed.

Dark, milk or white chocolate can be made into wonderful sweet or savoury dishes. The great taste of chocolate is down to its cocoa content, the higher the percentage of cocoa the richer, stronger and more bitter the flavour. Using good quality chocolate you can create a fantastic range of flavours: tarts that melt in the mouth; chocolate truffles that are silky and smooth; intensely rich and decadent sauces; or delicate and light mousses.

This wonderful ancient ingredient can be paired with fruits, nuts, meats and cheese, so we have put together some of our favourite recipes to show you how versatile chocolate is and how to create fantastic results in your own kitchen. We hope our recipes bring you the pleasure they have to us.

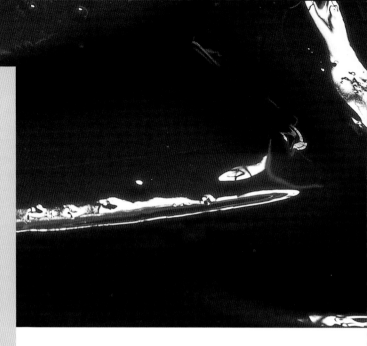

Types of chocolate

When choosing chocolate to cook with, opt for one with a high percentage of cocoa solids and no more than 31 per cent cocoa butter. Bear in mind that over 75 per cent cocoa solids gives an extra bitter, very dark chocolate that some people find unpalatable.

Plain chocolate, with a cocoa solids content of between 55 and 75 per cent, has a rich, full taste and the majority of the recipes in this book use a chocolate that falls within this range. It is advisable to always buy the best quality you can find, and generally the higher the cocoa content the more expensive the chocolate will be.

Couverture chocolate is a plain, dark chocolate containing a proportion of cocoa butter (about 31 per cent), which makes it easier to work with. It is often called "dipping" or "coating" chocolate and is commonly used for confectionery and decorations.

Milk chocolate has added milk solids or cream and sugar. Quality varies so again it is best to buy a more expensive brand and avoid those with added vegetable fat.

White chocolate is technically not chocolate at all but a combination of cocoa butter, milk solids and sugar.

Melting Chocolate

Chocolate should be melted carefully and gently. If overheated it can scorch or if it comes into contact with water or steam can "seize" when it hardens into a lump making it unworkable.

Firstly, break the chocolate into small, even-sized pieces or use pistoles (buttons), place in a heatproof bowl that is clean and dry. Place the bowl over a saucepan half-filled with gently simmering water. (The bowl should not touch the water.) The heat should be at its lowest setting or turned off. Stir frequently to keep the temperature steady until the chocolate is melted.

Tempering

Tempering is a method of melting and cooling chocolate to a certain temperature so that when it cools it has a glossy lustre and a great "snap" when broken. Tempering is necessary when making filled chocolates, chocolate decorations or coating but make sure you use good quality chocolate. It is best to work in a cool, dry environment.

A simple way to temper chocolate is to melt the chocolate following the method on page 7 until it reaches a temperature of 45°C/115°F. Remove the bowl from the heat then pour two-thirds on to a dry marble slab or work surface. Using a palette knife, spread the chocolate back and fourth until it thickens and is on the point of setting. Transfer the chocolate from the marble to the reserved melted chocolate and stir until combined.

Chocolate decorations

Bubble wrap chocolate

This is a simple yet stunning way to decorate desserts and cakes.

100g (3¹/₂oz) plain chocolate, broken into pieces

1 Melt the chocolate in a heatproof bowl placed over a saucepan of gently simmering water.

2 Place a 15cm (6in) square sheet of plastic bubble wrap (bubble-side up) on a baking sheet. Pour the melted chocolate over the sheet and spread out using a palette knife. Chill until set. Carefully remove the plastic from the chocolate then break into pieces the desired size.

Making chocolate curls and shavings

Decorative curls can be made from chocolate that is at room temperature. Use a vegetable peeler to shave the sides of a block or bar of white, milk or plain chocolate. For shavings, use chilled chocolate and follow the method above.

White and milk chocolate garnish

Swirls of melted white chocolate over milk chocolate (or you could use plain) give a highly decorative effect. Leave to set in sheets then break into pieces the desired size.

250g (9oz) milk or plain chocolate, broken into pieces
50g (1³/₄oz) white chocolate, broken into pieces

1 Melt the milk chocolate in a heatproof bowl placed over a saucepan of gently simmering water. Repeat this method with the white chocolate.

2 Line a baking sheet with baking parchment. Pour the milk chocolate over the sheet and spread out evenly using a palette knife.

3 Using a spoon, drizzle the white chocolate over the dark chocolate in a liberal pattern. Chill until set then break into pieces. Chill until ready to use.

Chocolate filigree

Ornamental shapes and decorations add the finishing touch to desserts and cakes.

30g (5 tbsp) plain flour
60g (¹/₂ cup) icing sugar
50g (scant ¹/₂ cup) cocoa powder
50g (scant ¹/₄ cup) egg whites

1 Preheat the oven to 190°C (375°F). Line a large baking sheet with baking parchment. Sift the flour, icing sugar and cocoa powder together into a mixing bowl then beat in the egg whites.

2 Spoon the chocolate mixture into a piping bag then cut a small hole at the end. Pipe the mixture into your desired design on to the baking parchment.

3 Bake for 3–4 minutes until set. Remove from the oven and leave the decorations to cool slightly then carefully transfer to a wire rack to cool.

Piped chocolate decorations

Melted chocolate can be piped into decorative patterns to enhance desserts and special occasion cakes.

For this, gently pour cooled melted or tempered chocolate into a baking parchment piping bag or small plastic piping bag and cut a very small piece off the end.

Use as desired, or if it is your first attempt it is advisable to draw a pattern on to a sheet of baking parchment then trace over the top with the piped chocolate. Leave to set, either at room temperature or chill. Carefully remove from the paper using a palette knife.

Hot puddings

Banana and chocolate soufflé pancakes

THESE MOREISH PANCAKES ARE VERY STRAIGHTFORWARD TO MAKE. THE FILLING IS EXTREMELY LIGHT AND AIRY WITH THE ADDED BONUS OF MELTED CHOCOLATE.

Ingredients

125g (1 heaped cup) plain flour
a pinch of salt
1 free-range egg, lightly beaten
15g (1 tablespoon) unsalted butter, melted
300ml (1¼ cups) milk
light olive oil or sunflower oil, for frying
icing sugar, for dusting

For the filling:

8 free-range egg whites
50g (¼ cup) caster sugar
1 quantity crème pâtissiere (see page 18)
200g (7oz) plain chocolate, broken into pieces
4 bananas, sliced

Serves 6

1 To make the pancakes, sift the flour and salt into a mixing bowl. Make a well in the centre and whisk in the whole eggs, butter and half the milk. Whisk to make a smooth batter, then mix in the remaining milk. Leave the batter to rest for 20 minutes.

2 Preheat the oven to 220°C (427°F). Heat a 18cm (7in) non-stick frying pan to a high temperature – you should feel the heat rising. Pour in 1 teaspoon of oil and swirl it around the pan. Ladle 2–3 tablespoons of batter into the frying pan and swirl it around until it coats the base of the pan. Cook until light golden, about 1½ minutes, then flip it over and cook for a further 45 seconds. Transfer to a plate. Repeat this process to make 12 pancakes in total.

3 To make the soufflé, whisk the egg whites until they form soft peaks. Add the caster sugar, a little at a time, and whisk until the mixture forms stiff peaks. Whisk half the egg white mixture into the crème pâtissiere then fold in the remaining mixture using a metal spoon.

4 Place a pancake on a baking tray and top one half with a good spoonful of the soufflé mixture, leaving a gap around the edge, then place a few slices of banana and some chocolate pieces on top. Fold the other half of the pancake over and repeat with the remaining pancakes. Bake for 8–10 minutes. Serve 2 pancakes per person, dusting the tops with icing sugar.

Chocolate fondant

TAKE CARE NOT TO OVERCOOK THESE LIGHT CHOCOLATE PUDDINGS – THE CENTRES SHOULD OOZE WHEN CUT INTO.

Ingredients

125g (4½oz) plain chocolate, broken into pieces
125g (9 tablespoons) unsalted butter, plus extra for greasing
4 free-range eggs
75g (6 tbsp) caster sugar
50g (½ cup) self-raising flour, plus extra for dusting
1 tbsp cocoa powder, plus extra for dusting
whipped cream, to serve (optional)

Serves 6

1 Melt the chocolate and butter together in a heatproof bowl placed over a saucepan of gently simmering water. Stir until combined then leave to cool.

2 Preheat the oven to 180°C (350°F) and lightly butter and flour 6 x 200ml (scant 1 cup) pudding basins. Whisk the eggs and sugar together until light and pale and doubled in volume.

3 Fold the egg mixture into the cooled chocolate. Sift in the flour and cocoa then fold until combined.

4 Spoon the chocolate mixture into the prepared pudding basins and bake for 6–7 minutes until risen. Loosen the puddings with a knife and carefully turn out. Dust with cocoa powder and serve with whipped cream, if using.

Previous page: Banana and chocolate soufflé pancakes
Opposite: Chocolate fondant

Ingredients

25g (2 tablespoons) caster sugar
50ml ($^1/_4$ cup) water
250g (9oz) white chocolate, broken into pieces
30ml (2 tbsp) almond liqueur
4 free-range egg yolks
juice and zest of 2 mandarins
30ml (2 tbsp) orange liqueur
150ml ($^2/_3$ cup) whipping cream
25g ($^1/_4$ cup) icing sugar
1 vanilla pod, split and seeds scraped out
4 pieces of plain chocolate garnish (see page 9)
clotted cream, to serve

For the spiced bread:
1 free-range egg, lightly beaten
150ml ($^2/_3$ cup) milk
30ml (2 tbsp) single cream
40g (scant $^1/_2$ cup) icing sugar
25g (2 tbsp) butter
200g (7oz) spiced bread (pain d'epice) or brioche, about
6 x 6cm ($2^1/_2$in) x 5cm (2in) thick slices

Serves 6

1 Heat the sugar and water in a small saucepan, stirring, until the sugar dissolves. Bring the mixture to the boil and cook until it becomes syrupy. Set aside to cool.

2 Melt the chocolate in a heatproof bowl placed over a saucepan of gently simmering water – take care not to overheat the chocolate as it can separate. Leave to cool.

3 Put the sugar syrup, almond liqueur and egg yolks in a bowl placed over a saucepan of gently simmering water and whisk until light and fluffy. Remove from the heat and leave to cool. Fold the mixture into the melted chocolate. Add the mandarin juice and zest and stir in the orange liqueur.

4 Lightly whip the cream with the icing sugar and vanilla seeds then fold into the chocolate mixture.

5 To make the spiced bread, mix the egg with the milk, cream and icing sugar. Melt the butter in a frying pan. Dip each piece of bread into the cream mixture then fry until golden brown.

6 To serve, place a round of bread in the bottom of a shallow bowl, pour the chocolate soup over the top and brown under the grill (or use a blowtorch) for a few seconds. Top the bread with a piece of chocolate and serve with a scoop of clotted cream.

White chocolate and mandarin soup with spiced bread

WE WERE GIVEN THIS RECIPE BY OUR GOOD FRIEND ADAM NEWELL, WHO IS CHEF/PATRON AT ZIBIBBO IN WELLINGTON, NEW ZEALAND. THE "SOUP" IS LIGHT, FLUFFY AND VERY RICH AND GOES REALLY WELL WITH THE SPICED BREAD. TOP WITH CLOTTED CREAM.

1 Preheat the oven to 180°C (350°F). Lightly butter 4 large ramekins or ovenproof mugs and set aside.

2 Break the brioche into small pieces and divide between the ramekins or mugs.

3 Gently heat the milk with the vanilla pod and seeds, add 150g (5½oz) of the chocolate and stir until it melts.

4 Whisk together the eggs and sugar then add the chocolate milk, stirring well.

5 Divide the remaining chocolate between the ramekins or mugs, pour over the hot chocolate milk and press the brioche down so that it absorbs the liquid. Leave to stand for 2 minutes.

6 Put the ramekins or mugs in a roasting tin. Pour in enough hot water to come two-thirds of the way up the sides of the ramekins or mugs. Bake for 30–40 minutes then leave to rest for 10 minutes. Serve with a good spoonful of clotted or whipped cream, if using. (You can also turn the puddings out of the ramekins or mugs.)

Chocolate brioche butter pudding

THIS TAKE ON THE CLASSIC BREAD AND BUTTER PUDDING USES BRIOCHE AND CHOCOLATE, WHICH GIVES IT REAL GUTS. A DOLLOP OF CLOTTED CREAM FINISHES IT OFF TO PERFECTION!

Ingredients
butter, for greasing
200g (7oz) brioche, about 6 slices
600ml (2½ cups) milk
1 vanilla pod, split and seeds scraped out
200g (7oz) plain chocolate, broken into pieces
4 free-range eggs
25g (2 tbsp) caster sugar
clotted or whipped cream, to serve (optional)

Serves 4

1 Preheat the oven to 180°C (350°F). Line a 30cm (12in) square x 5cm (2in) deep baking tin with baking parchment.

2 Melt the chocolate and butter together in a heatproof bowl placed over a saucepan of gently simmering water. Stir well until the chocolate and butter are mixed together. Dissolve the coffee in 1 tablespoon water then stir into the chocolate mixture.

3 Using an electric hand whisk, whisk the eggs and sugar together in a heatproof bowl placed over a pan of gently simmering water until doubled in volume. (This is called a sabayon and it is ready when light and pale and the mixture holds a ribbon trail for 4 seconds when the whisk is lifted.)

4 Remove from the heat and gently fold in the chocolate mixture. Sift in the flour a little at a time, folding it in as you go. Finally, fold in the nuts.

5 Spoon the chocolate mixture into the prepared baking tin, level the top and bake for 25–30 minutes until risen. Leave to cool slightly then cut into squares. Serve warm with cream or ice cream, if liked.

Chocolate brownies

THIS CLASSIC CHOCOLATE BROWNIE RECIPE COMES FROM OUR TIME IN NEW YORK – EVERY BITE BRINGS BACK HAPPY MEMORIES.

Ingredients
550g (1lb 3oz) plain chocolate, broken into pieces
325g (11½oz) unsalted butter, cut into pieces
1 tbsp instant coffee granules
5 large free-range eggs
325g (1⅔ cups) caster sugar
175g (1½ cups) plain flour
100g (scant 1 cup) walnuts, chopped
100g (scant 1 cup) macadamia nuts, chopped
cream or vanilla ice cream, to serve (optional)

Makes about 16

Pictured on page 2

1 Put the milk, half of the sugar and vanilla pod and seeds in a saucepan and gently warm. Remove from the heat and leave to infuse for 15 minutes.

2 In a mixing bowl, whisk together the egg yolks, the flour and the remaining sugar until it forms a smooth paste.

3 Pour the milk over and mix well. Transfer to a clean pan and heat gently for 10–15 minutes, stirring continuously, until the mixture begins to thicken. Transfer to a clean bowl, cover with clingfilm and leave to cool.

4 Preheat the oven to 200°C (400°F). Brush the insides of 6 large ramekin dishes with soft butter – always brush up the sides. Add a tablespoon of sugar to each ramekin and tilt and rotate until the inside is coated in the sugar. Pour out any excess sugar then chill.

5 Whisk the egg whites until they form stiff peaks. Put the crème pâtissiere into a large bowl and whisk well. Add half the egg whites and whisk well until the mixture forms a smooth paste. Add the remaining egg whites and fold in with a large metal spoon.

6 Spoon the soufflé mixture into the prepared ramekins, filling them up to the top. Carefully tap down the dishes (this releases any trapped air). Place on a baking tray and bake for 10–15 minutes – do not open the oven door during cooking since this allows the hot air to escape.

7 Meanwhile, make the chocolate sauce. Gently bring the cream up to the boil. Pour on to the chocolate and stir until melted. Set aside.

8 When the soufflés are ready, carefully but quickly remove from the oven. Dust with cocoa powder and serve immediately with the chocolate sauce.

Ingredients

For the crème pâtissiere:
475ml (2 cups) milk
125g (heaped 1/2 cup) caster sugar, plus extra for dusting
1 vanilla pod, split and seeds scraped out
6 free-range eggs, separated
60g (1/2 cup) plain flour
softened butter, for greasing

For the chocolate sauce:
350ml (1 1/2 cups) whipping cream
150g (5 1/2oz) plain chocolate
cocoa powder, for dusting

Serves 6

Vanilla soufflé with chocolate sauce

A SUPERB, BREATH-TAKING DESSERT WITH A GUARANTEED WOW FACTOR. THE SECRETS TO A GOOD SOUFFLÉ ARE A WELL BUTTERED AND SUGARED DISH, THE CRÈME PÂTISSIERE SHOULD ALWAYS BE AT ROOM TEMPERATURE AND THE MIXING BOWL METICULOUSLY CLEAN AND, MOST IMPORTANTLY, GOOD COMPANY TO SHARE IT WITH.

Ice creams and chilled desserts

Dark chocolate ice cream

THERE IS NOTHING BETTER THAN THE TASTE OF HOMEMADE ICE CREAM, AND THIS RECIPE IS RICH AND EXTREMELY MOREISH.

Ingredients
2 free-range eggs, plus 2 additional yolks
125g (heaped 1/2 cup) caster sugar
300ml (1 1/4 cups) double cream
200g (7oz) plain chocolate, broken into pieces
300ml (1 1/4 cups) whipping cream

Makes about 750ml (3 cups)

1 Whisk the eggs, additional yolks and sugar together until light and pale.

2 Put the double cream into a saucepan and bring up to the boil. Pour the cream over the chocolate and stir until it is melted. Leave to cool.

3 When cool, pour the chocolate and cream into the egg mixture. Pour into a clean saucepan and heat gently, stirring constantly, until the mixture is thick enough to coat the back of a wooden spoon; do not allow it to boil or the mixture will curdle. Pass through a fine sieve into a bowl and leave to cool.

4 Fold the chocolate mixture into the whipping cream. Pour the mixture into an ice cream maker and churn then freeze. If making by hand, pour the mixture into a freezer-proof container then freeze for 40 minutes. Remove from the freezer, whisk to break up any ice crystals then refreeze. Repeat this process for the next 2 1/2 hours then freeze until firm.

5 Leave the ice cream to soften for 5–10 minutes then serve in scoops.

Chocolate mousse

WE HAVE EXPERIMENTED WITH MANY MOUSSE RECIPES AND AGREE THAT THIS IS ONE OF THE MOST DELICIOUS AND SIMPLE TO MAKE.

Ingredients
150g (5 1/2oz) plain chocolate, broken into pieces
5 free-range egg whites
175ml (3/4 cup) whipping cream, whipped
cocoa powder and icing sugar, for dusting

Serves 4

1 Melt the chocolate in a heatproof bowl placed over a saucepan of gently simmering water. Leave to cool slightly.

2 Whisk the egg whites until they form soft peaks then fold into the chocolate. Fold the whipped cream into the chocolate mixture. Chill until set.

3 To serve, dust each serving plate with cocoa powder and icing sugar then shape the mousse between 2 warm dessertspoons into a quenelle or egg-shaped portion. Place 3 quenelles on each plate and serve. Alternatively, spoon the mousse into tall glasses and chill until set.

Previous page: Dark chocolate ice cream
Opposite: Chocolate mousse

White chocolate and chilli ice cream

THE MOUTH-TINGLING, CLEAN FLAVOUR OF THE RED CHILLI WORKS WELL WITH THE WHITE CHOCOLATE IN THIS BRILLIANT AND UNUSUAL ICE CREAM THAT HAS BECOME A BIG FAVOURITE AT OUR RESTAURANT.

1 Bring the water to the boil in a saucepan. Add 1 tablespoon of the caster sugar and chilli then reduce the heat and simmer for 5 minutes until it becomes a light syrup. Remove from the heat and allow to cool.

2 Put the cream, milk and vanilla pod in a saucepan and bring up to the boil. Remove from the heat and allow to infuse and cool.

3 Melt the chocolate in a heatproof bowl placed over a saucepan of gently simmering water. Leave to cool.

4 Whisk the egg yolks with the rest of the sugar until light and fluffy. Pour the infused milk into the egg mixture and stir with a spatula. Pour the mixture into a clean pan and heat gently, stirring continuously, until it is thick enough to coat the back of a wooden spoon: do not allow it to boil or the mixture will curdle. Remove the vanilla pod and pass the mixture through a fine sieve into a bowl. Fold in the white chocolate.

5 Pour the mixture into an ice cream maker, churn, and when the ice cream starts to freeze add the chilli mixture, churn for a further 2 minutes then freeze. If making by hand, pour the mixture into a freezer-proof container then freeze for 40 minutes. Remove from the freezer, whisk to break up any ice crystals, stir in the chilli mixture, then refreeze. Repeat this process for the next 2$\frac{1}{2}$ hours then freeze until firm.

6 Leave the ice cream to soften for 5–10 minutes then serve in scoops.

Ingredients

60ml (4 tbsp) water
200g (1 cup) caster sugar
10g (2 tsp) seeded and finely diced red chilli
400ml (1$\frac{2}{3}$ cups) double cream
400ml (1$\frac{2}{3}$ cups) semi-skimmed milk
1 vanilla pod, split
300g (11oz) white chocolate, broken into pieces
8 free-range egg yolks

Makes about 1 litre (4 cups)

Chocolate arlequin

THE LAYERS OF RICH WHITE AND DARK CHOCOLATE MOUSSE MAKE
THIS FRENCH-INSPIRED DESSERT A MUST FOR CHOCOLATE LOVERS.

1 Preheat the oven to 180°C (350°F). Line a 25cm (10in) x
20cm (8in) x 5cm (2in) deep baking tray with baking
parchment, then butter and flour.

2 To make the sponge, whisk the eggs and caster sugar
together until light and pale. Sift the flour into the bowl
then fold in carefully with a spatula. Pour into the prepared
baking tray, level with a palette knife, and bake for 20–25
minutes until risen and golden. Remove from the oven and
leave the sponge in the tin for 10 minutes then turn out
on to a wire rack to cool.

3 Next, to make the plain chocolate cream, melt the
chocolate in a heatproof bowl placed over a saucepan of
gently simmering water, then set aside to cool slightly. Fold
the crème pâtissiere into the melted plain chocolate then
fold in the whipped cream. Repeat this method to make
the white chocolate cream.

4 Trim the edges of the sponge base then slice horizontally.
Using a 7$\frac{1}{2}$cm (3$\frac{1}{2}$in) flan ring cut the sponge into 16 x
1cm ($\frac{1}{2}$in) thick rounds. Put a sponge base into the
bottom of one of 8 individual flan rings. Drizzle over a little
of the brandy. Spoon over the dark chocolate cream until
the mould is half full. Place a second layer of sponge on
top. Gently push down then fill the mould with the white
chocolate cream and smooth the top. Repeat to make
seven more desserts then chill for 4–6 hours.

5 Remove the flan rings with the aid of a kitchen
blowtorch or wrap a hot tea towel around the ring. If liked,
gently mottle the top of each dessert with a blowtorch. If
using a blowtorch, return the desserts to the fridge to chill.
Serve decorated with orange segments, shaved white
chocolate and fresh mint.

Ingredients
butter, for greasing
250g (2$\frac{1}{4}$ cups) plain flour, plus extra for dusting
8 free-range eggs
250g (1$\frac{1}{4}$ cups) caster sugar
$\frac{1}{2}$ tsp vanilla extract
25ml (1$\frac{1}{2}$ tbsp) brandy

For the dark chocolate cream:
175g (6oz) plain chocolate, broken into pieces
$\frac{1}{2}$ quantity crème pâtissiere (see page 18)
325ml (scant 1$\frac{1}{2}$ cups) whipping cream, whipped

For the white chocolate cream:
175g (6oz) white chocolate, broken into pieces
$\frac{1}{2}$ quantity crème pâtissiere (see page 18)
325ml (scant 1$\frac{1}{2}$ cups) whipping cream, whipped

To decorate:
orange segments
white chocolate shavings (see page 8)
fresh mint leaves

Serves 8

Something chocolate

SINCE OPENING TANNERS IN 1999, THIS RECIPE REMAINS A FIRM
FAVOURITE. IT REALLY IS VERY SIMPLE TO PREPARE AND IS BEST LEFT
AT ROOM TEMPERATURE FOR A FEW MINUTES BEFORE YOU SERVE.

Ingredients
125g (4$^{1}/_{2}$oz) plain chocolate, broken into pieces
125g (4$^{1}/_{2}$oz) milk chocolate, broken into pieces
250ml (1 cup) whipping cream

To serve:
1 mango, peeled, stoned and finely chopped
150g (1 cup) raspberries
3 tbsp melted plain chocolate
4 small pieces of bubble wrap chocolate (see page 8)

Serves 4

1 Melt both types of chocolate in a heatproof bowl placed
over a saucepan of gently simmering water. Leave to
slightly cool.

2 Half whip the cream – do not whip to a full peak as the
cream needs to be carefully folded into the chocolate –
then fold into the chocolate until combined.

3 Spoon the chocolate mixture into 4 paper cones (like the
ones used in water dispensers) or 7$^{1}/_{2}$cm (3in) ramekins,
tap to remove any excess air and smooth over the top. If
you are using the paper cones, place each one in a plastic
cup to keep it upright. Refrigerate the cones or ramekins
until the chocolate is set; this will take about 3 hours.

4 Meanwhile, make the fruit sauces. Put the mango in a
blender and process until puréed. Press the mango sauce
through a sieve to remove any fibres. Repeat this process
to make the raspberry sauce.

5 To remove the chocolate from the cones, quickly
submerge each cone in warm water and carefully unpeel.
To serve, place a cone or ramekin in the centre of each
serving plate, paint strips of melted chocolate on the plate
and drizzle with the mango and raspberry sauces. Finally,
place a piece of bubble wrap chocolate on top of each
cone or ramekin.

Chocolate bavarois

THIS REVIVED CLASSIC IS POPULAR IN OUR RESTAURANT. IT HAS A
BLANCMANGE-TYPE TEXTURE AND LOOKS GOOD DECORATED WITH PIPED CREAM.

Ingredients
light olive oil, for greasing
3 free-range eggs, separated
50g (3½ tbsp) caster sugar
250ml (1 cup) milk
1 vanilla pod, split and seeds scraped out (optional)
3 gelatine leaves, soaked in water
60g (2oz) plain or milk chocolate, broken into pieces
275ml (scant 1¼ cups) whipping cream, plus extra
   to decorate
chocolate pistoles or buttons, to decorate
cocoa powder, for dusting

Serves 6

1 Lightly oil 6 x 150ml (²/₃ cup) pudding basins. In a mixing bowl, whisk the egg yolks and sugar together until light and fluffy.

2 Put the milk and vanilla pod and seeds, if using, in a saucepan and bring up to the boil. Pour the milk into the egg mixture, stir, and transfer the mixture to a clean pan. Heat gently, stirring continuously, until the mixture thickens enough to coat the back of a wooden spoon; do not allow to boil or the mixture will curdle. Remove the vanilla pod.

3 Squeeze the soaked gelatine leaves to remove any excess water and add to the custard mixture. Stir until the gelatine dissolves.

4 Pass the custard through a fine sieve into a bowl containing the chocolate. Stir well until the chocolate is melted. Allow the mixture to cool; this is best achieved when placed over a bowl of iced water.

5 Whisk the egg whites until they form soft peaks then whisk in the cream.

6 The chocolate mixture will start to set after a few minutes. At this point, gently fold in the egg white mixture; do not whisk as you do not want air bubbles in the bavarois. Pour the mixture into the prepared pudding basins and chill for 3–4 hours until set.

7 To serve, briefly place the basins in hot water. Carefully loosen the sides of the bavarois from the basins and turn out. Decorate the base with piped whipped cream, chocolate pistoles or buttons and dust with cocoa.

White chocolate mousse with passion fruit ripple

THIS INDULGENT MOUSSE IS SO LIGHT AND FLUFFY AND IS JUST AS DELICIOUS WITH CRUSHED FRESH RASPBERRIES OR BLACKBERRIES SWIRLED IN.

Ingredients
250g (9oz) white chocolate, broken into pieces
75ml (5 tbsp) milk
1 vanilla pod, split and seeds scraped out
3 free-range eggs, separated
350ml (1$^1/_2$ cups) whipping cream, whipped
4 passion fruit, halved and seeds scooped out
shredded fresh mint, to decorate (optional)

Serves 6

1 Put the chocolate and milk in a heatproof bowl placed over a saucepan of gently simmering water. Heat until the chocolate is just melted, stirring regularly. Stir the vanilla seeds into the mixture then leave to cool for 5 minutes.

2 Next, add the egg yolks, one at a time, beating well between each addition.

3 Fold the whipped cream into the chocolate mixture.

4 Whisk the egg whites until they form soft peaks, then fold half into the chocolate mixture, followed by the remaining half.

5 Divide the mousse between 6 individual serving bowls, then swirl the passion fruit pulp over the top of each bowl. Cover and chill for 3–4 hours until set. Decorate with mint before serving.

Chocolate tiramisu

THIS IS OUR BRASSERIE-STYLE VERSION OF THE CLASSIC ITALIAN DESSERT. SERVE IN INDIVIDUAL GLASSES OR FAMILY-STYLE SPOONED FROM A LARGE BOWL.

Ingredients
80g (6 tbsp) caster sugar
100ml (6$^1/_2$ tbsp) water
60ml (4 tbsp) Madeira
200g (7oz) plain chocolate, broken into pieces
200g (7oz) milk chocolate, broken into pieces
6 free-range eggs, separated
1kg (2lb 4oz) mascarpone
400g (14oz) Madeira cake, broken into pieces or cubed
cocoa powder, for dusting

Serves 6–8

1 Put half of the sugar and water in a small saucepan and bring to the boil, stir in the Madeira then leave to cool.

2 Melt the plain and milk chocolate in a heatproof bowl placed over a saucepan of gently simmering water. Leave to cool slightly.

3 Whisk the egg yolks and remaining caster sugar together until light and fluffy. Beat in the mascarpone until combined. Carefully fold the mascarpone mixture into the melted chocolate.

4 Whisk the egg whites until they form soft peaks then fold into the chocolate mixture.

5 Place half the Madeira cake in the bottom of serving glasses or in a large serving bowl. Pour half the Madeira syrup over the cake. Cover the sponge with the mascarpone mixture. Repeat with another layer of cake, syrup and mascarpone.

6 Chill then dust with cocoa powder before serving.

Pictured on page 1

Chocolate marquise

DURING THE SUMMER MONTHS WE ARE INUNDATED WITH FRESH BERRIES FROM THE TAMAR VALLEY, NEAR US HERE IN PLYMOUTH, DEVON. YOU CAN USE RASPBERRIES, BLACKCURRANTS, STRAWBERRIES OR BLUEBERRIES – OR A MIX OF EVERYTHING – AS PART OF THE FILLING IN THIS DECADENT CHOCOLATE SWISS ROLL.

1 Preheat the oven to 180°C (350°F). Press half of the raspberries through a sieve or purée in a blender to make a smooth sauce. If blending, press through a sieve afterwards to remove the seeds.

2 In a clean mixing bowl, whisk the egg yolks with half of the icing sugar until light and fluffy. In a separate bowl, whisk the egg whites until they form soft peaks then gradually add the remaining sugar and whisk until stiff. Stir the two egg mixtures together using a metal spoon. Add the cornflour and cocoa powder and fold until combined.

3 Line a 26cm (10½in) x 24cm (9½in) baking tray with baking parchment, then grease lightly with butter and dust with flour. Spread the roulade mixture in an even layer, about 1cm (½in) thick, to cover the base of the tray. Bake for 8–12 minutes until risen and the mixture springs back when pressed – do not worry if it feels slightly soft as it needs to be for rolling later.

4 Turn the roulade out on to a clean, damp tea towel; carefully remove the paper (if this proves difficult, dampen the paper with a little water and carefully peel off) and neatly trim the edges.

5 Allow the roulade to cool slightly. Smear the raspberry sauce (setting some aside to serve) over the roulade, then top with the whipped cream and level with a palette knife. Liberally scatter the raspberries (setting some aside to serve) over the cream. Now comes the fun bit!

6 Very carefully, from the short end, roll up the roulade using the damp tea towel as a guide. Leave the roulade wrapped in the tea towel and set aside to chill.

7 When you are ready to serve, carefully remove the tea towel and slice the roulade on the diagonal. Serve with the reserved raspberries and raspberry sauce and decorate with fresh mint.

Ingredients

200g (1¼ cups) raspberries
6 free-range eggs, separated
250g (2¼ cups) icing sugar, sifted
25g (4 tbsp) cornflour, sifted
100g (scant 1 cup) cocoa powder, sifted
butter, for greasing
flour, for dusting
300ml (1¼ cups) whipping cream, whipped
fresh mint leaves, to decorate

Serves 10

Chocolate and ginger terrine with cinnamon custard

A SIMPLE CLASSIC COMBINATION OF CHOCOLATE TRUFFLE WITH STEM GINGER, SERVED WITH A PERFUMED, LIGHT CINNAMON CUSTARD. A GREAT MARRIAGE!

Ingredients

For the terrine:
250g (9oz) plain chocolate, broken into pieces
250g (9oz) milk chocolate, broken into pieces
2 pieces of stem ginger in syrup, finely chopped
500ml (2¼ cups) whipping cream, whipped

For the custard:
500ml (2¼ cups) milk
1 vanilla pod, split and seeds scraped out
100g (½ cup) caster sugar
6 free-range egg yolks
1 tsp ground cinnamon

Serves 6

1 Melt the plain and milk chocolate together in a heatproof bowl placed over a saucepan of gently simmering water. Mix in the chopped stem ginger then allow to cool slightly. Fold the whipped cream into the chocolate mixture.

2 Line a 450g (1lb) loaf tin or small terrine mould with clingfilm. Pour the chocolate mixture into the prepared tin or mould. Cover and chill in the fridge for at least 3 hours until set.

3 To make the custard, heat the milk with the vanilla pod and seeds and half of the sugar up to boiling point, stirring occasionally. Meanwhile, whisk the egg yolks with the remaining sugar and cinnamon until light and fluffy.

4 Whisk the hot milk into the egg mixture and return it to the saucepan. Heat gently, stirring continuously, until the custard thickens enough to coat the back of a wooden spoon; do not allow it to boil or the mixture will curdle. Pass through a fine sieve then cool and chill.

5 To serve, gently turn out the terrine, carefully remove the clingfilm and slice using a hot knife. Place a slice of the terrine on a serving plate and drizzle around the custard.

Chef's note: To serve the terrine in the chocolate box, pictured, melt 250g (9oz) plain chocolate following the instructions for White and milk chocolate garnish, page 9. Before serving each slice of the terrine, use a hot knife to cut the chocolate into rectangles the appropriate size. Prop the chocolate around the terrine slice and pipe chocolate into the corners and around the base of the box to secure.

Cakes and pastries

Dark chocolate truffle cake

THIS IS ONE OF THE FIRST DESSERTS
WE MADE WHEN WE STARTED IN A
PROFESSIONAL KITCHEN. SIMPLICITY
ON A PLATE – MILK AND PLAIN CHOCOLATE
WITH WHIPPED CREAM – SMOOTH, RICH
AND CREAMY. PURE INDULGENCE!

Ingredients
225g (8oz) plain chocolate, broken into pieces
300ml (1¼ cups) thick double cream
cocoa powder, for dusting

Serves 4–6

1 Melt the chocolate in a heatproof bowl placed over a saucepan of gently simmering water.

2 Gently heat the cream then stir it into the melted chocolate.

3 Pour the mixture into a 20cm (8in) loose-bottomed, non-stick flan ring on a flat plate and leave to set for 3 hours in the refrigerator.

4 To remove the ring, heat the edges with a blowtorch for 30 seconds or dip a thin, bladed knife in boiling water and run it around the inside of the ring. Use the back of the knife to smooth the edges. Dust with cocoa powder.

Dark chocolate and marmalade tart

THIS IMPRESSIVE TART HAS A FANTASTIC
COMBINATION OF FLAVOURS: THE
MARMALADE WORKS EXCEPTIONALLY WELL
WITH THE CHOCOLATE, WHILE THE
MASCARPONE ADDS A RICH CREAMINESS.

Ingredients
250g (2¼ cups) plain flour, sifted
100g (7 tbsp) cold unsalted butter, diced, plus extra for greasing
100g (scant 1 cup) icing sugar, sifted
2 free-range egg yolks
4 drops vanilla extract
cocoa powder, for dusting
mascarpone and pieces of Milk and white chocolate decoration (see page 9), to decorate

For the filling:
200g (scant 1 cup) unsalted butter, cubed
300g (10½ oz) plain chocolate, broken into pieces
60g (¼ cup) caster sugar
2 free-range eggs, plus 2 additional egg yolks
150g (½ cup) thick-cut marmalade

Serve 4–6

1 First make the sweet pastry case, place the flour and butter in a food processor and process until fine crumbs. Transfer to a mixing bowl and mix in the icing sugar.

2 Beat the egg yolks and vanilla extract together in a bowl and add to the pastry mixture. Bring the pastry together, wrap in clingfilm and allow to rest in the fridge for 1 hour.

3 Preheat the oven to 180°C (350°F). Grease a 23cm (9in) loose-bottomed flan tin. Remove the pastry from the fridge, roll out, then press the pastry into the tin. Chill for 20 minutes. Trim the edges then line the pastry with baking parchment, fill with baking beans and bake blind for 15–20 minutes or until the sides of the pastry are golden. Remove the parchment and beans and allow to cool. Reduce the oven to 160°C (325°F).

4 To make the filling, melt the butter and chocolate together in a heatproof bowl placed over a saucepan of gently simmering water, stir until combined. Whisk together the sugar, eggs and additional egg yolks then fold into the chocolate mixture.

5 Spoon the marmalade into the pastry case and spread out evenly. Pour the chocolate mixture into the case, level, and bake for 15 minutes. Remove the tart from the oven and cool on a wire rack. Dust the tart with cocoa powder then remove from the tin. To serve, slice the tart with a hot knife and top each slice with a spoonful of mascarpone and a piece of milk and white chocolate.

Previous page: Dark chocolate truffle cake
Opposite: Dark chocolate and marmalade tart

1 Preheat the oven to 220°C (425°F). Lightly grease a 6-hole, non-stick muffin tin.

2 Put the egg yolks, sugar and cornflour into a bowl and whisk until light and fluffy. Add the cream and water then whisk again. Pour the mixture into a saucepan with the vanilla pod and seeds. Heat over a medium heat, stirring continuously with a wooden spoon, for about 5 minutes until the mixture thickens.

3 Remove from the heat, add the chocolate and stir until the chocolate is melted. Leave to cool.

4 Roll out the pastry on a floured work surface until 1cm ($^1/_2$in) thick. Using a pastry cutter, cut 6 x 10cm (4in) rounds then press each pastry round into a muffin tin hole. Place in a freezer and chill for 10 minutes.

5 Next, fold the pistachios into the chocolate custard. Remove the muffin tray from the freezer and divide the chocolate custard between the tart shells and smooth the tops. Bake for 20 minutes until the pastry is golden.

6 Remove from the oven and cool on a wire rack for 10 minutes before removing the tarts from the muffin trays. Sprinkle with additional pistachios before serving.

Ingredients

butter, for greasing
4 free-range egg yolks
60g ($^1/_4$ cup) caster sugar
15g (2 tbsp) cornflour
200ml (scant 1 cup) double cream
120ml ($^1/_2$ cup) water
1 vanilla pod, split and seeds scraped out
150g (5$^1/_2$oz) plain chocolate, grated
200g (7oz) sheet puff pastry
30g ($^1/_4$ cup) peeled and chopped pistachios, plus extra for sprinkling

Makes 6

Chocolate and pistachio custard tarts

THESE INDIVIDUAL TARTS WITH THEIR INTENSELY CHOCOLATEY CUSTARD, PISTACHIOS AND
RICH PASTRY SHELL MAKE THE PERFECT AFTERNOON TREAT.

Olivia's chocolate cake

ENJOY THIS IMPRESSIVE LAYERED CHOCOLATE CAKE – IT'S A MASSIVE
FAVOURITE WITH CHRIS'S ELDEST DAUGHTER, OLIVIA.

Ingredients
butter, for greasing
100g (³/₄ cup) plain flour, plus extra for dusting
150g (scant 1 cup) raspberries
4 free-range eggs
125g (heaped ¹/₂ cup) caster sugar
30g (¹/₄ cup) cocoa powder

For the chocolate cream:
500ml (2¹/₃ cups) whipping cream
30g (¹/₄ cup) cocoa powder
30g (¹/₄ cup) icing sugar

To decorate:
chocolate pistoles or buttons
piped chocolate (see page 9)
whipped cream

Serves 10

1 Preheat the oven to 180°C (350°F). Butter and flour a
25cm (10in) cake tin. To make the raspberry purée, blend
the raspberries in a blender or press through a sieve. If
blending, press through a sieve to remove any seeds.

2 In a bowl, whisk the eggs and caster sugar together until
light and pale. Sift the flour and cocoa powder into the
bowl then fold in carefully with a spatula. Pour into the
prepared cake tin and bake for 20–25 minutes until risen.
Remove from the oven and leave in the tin for 10 minutes
then turn out on to a wire rack to cool.

3 To make the chocolate cream, pour the whipping cream
into a bowl and sift in the cocoa powder and icing sugar
and whisk the mixture until thick and creamy.

4 Cut the cake into 3 horizontal layers, and place one layer
on a serving plate. Spoon half of the raspberry purée over
the cake, add a large spoonful of the chocolate cream and
spread it all over. Repeat with a second layer of sponge,
raspberry purée and cream.

5 Place the remaining layer of sponge on top and press
down gently. Using a palette knife, spread the remaining
chocolate cream around the sides of the cake and over the
top. Smooth and level the chocolate cream with a warm
palette knife.

6 To decorate, pipe chocolate cream and whipped cream
around the base and top of the cake. Pipe chocolate over
the cream then arrange chocolate pistoles or buttons on
top. Personalise the cake with piped chocolate, if liked (see
page 9).

Dreamy chocolate and orange cake

THE ULTIMATE COMBINATION OF CHOCOLATE AND ORANGE, THIS FOOLPROOF CAKE MAKES AN EXCELLENT DINNER PARTY DESSERT OR AFTERNOON TREAT.

Ingredients

250g (9oz) plain chocolate, broken into pieces
250g (heaped 1 cup) unsalted butter, cut into small pieces, plus extra for greasing
2 tbsp orange zest
6 free-range eggs, separated
125g (heaped $1/2$ cup) caster sugar
20g (3 tbsp) plain flour, sifted
25g ($1/4$ cup) ground almonds

To decorate:

cocoa powder, for dusting
orange slices and grated orange zest
mint leaves, torn
crème fraîche

Serves 6–8

1 Preheat the oven to 190°C (375°F). Lightly grease a 23cm (9in) spring-form cake tin. Melt the chocolate and butter with the orange zest in a heatproof bowl placed over a saucepan of gently simmering water. When just melted, stir the mixture and set aside.

2 Whisk the egg yolks with the sugar until light and fluffy. Gradually pour the melted chocolate into the egg mixture, stirring constantly. Next, take a large spoon and fold in the flour and ground almonds.

3 Put the egg whites into a clean bowl and whisk until they form stiff peaks. Using a large metal spoon, fold the egg whites into the chocolate mixture until they are just combined. Pour the mixture into the prepared tin and bake for 35 minutes – the cake will be very moist in the centre but avoid cooking it for any longer.

4 Remove the cake from the oven and leave to cool completely in the tin. Transfer the cake to a serving plate and dust with cocoa then decorate with orange slices and zest, fresh mint and spoonfuls of crème fraîche.

Chocolate and Devon blue cheese tart

BELIEVE IT OR NOT, CHOCOLATE AND BLUE CHEESE ARE A MATCH MADE IN HEAVEN
AS SHOWN IN THIS UNUSUAL BUT TRULY SUPERB, DECADENT DESSERT.

Ingredients

For the pastry:

250g (2$\frac{1}{4}$ cups) plain flour
$\frac{3}{4}$ tsp salt
1$\frac{1}{2}$ tsp icing sugar
125g (9 tbsp) unsalted butter, diced
1 free-range egg, lightly beaten
50ml ($\frac{1}{4}$ cup) water

For the filling:

200g (7oz) plain chocolate, broken into pieces
175g (10 tbsp) unsalted butter, melted
40g ($\frac{1}{3}$ cup) plain flour
3 free-range eggs
50g (scant $\frac{1}{4}$ cup) caster sugar
150g (1$\frac{1}{4}$ cups) Devon blue cheese or Stilton, crumbled

Serves 4

1 Sift the flour into a bowl then mix in the salt and icing sugar. Rub the butter into the flour until the mixture resembles fine breadcrumbs. Mix in the egg and water and form into a dough. Knead until smooth.

2 Lay out a large piece of clingfilm, place the dough on top, fold over the clingfilm and press the pastry out flat. Chill for 20 minutes. Lightly butter 4 x 10cm (4in) fluted, loose-bottomed flan tins.

3 On a floured work surface, roll out the pastry until about 3mm ($\frac{1}{8}$in) thick. Cut out 4 x 12cm (4$\frac{1}{2}$in) rounds and carefully press into the prepared flan tins, leaving any excess pastry overlapping the sides. Chill in the fridge for 20 minutes.

4 Meanwhile, preheat the oven to 180°C (350°F). To make the filling, gently melt the chocolate and butter together in a heatproof bowl placed over a saucepan of gently simmering water. Stir until combined then leave to cool.

5 Line the pastry cases with baking parchment, fill with baking beans and bake blind for 15–20 minutes or until the sides of the pastry are golden. Leave to cool on a wire rack. Remove the paper and beans from the tins then carefully trim the edges.

6 Increase the oven to 190°C (375°F). Whisk the eggs and sugar together until light and fluffy. Add the cooled chocolate and butter, then fold in the flour. Pour the mixture into the pastry moulds, almost up to the top. Sprinkle the cheese over the top then bake for 8–10 minutes. Leave to cool then carefully remove the tarts from the tins.

Petits fours

Chocolate tuiles

A PRETTY, CRISP PETIT FOUR THAT LOOKS
LIKE A CURVED TILE. SERVE AFTER A MEAL
WITH COFFEE OR AS AN ACCOMPANIMENT
TO A DESSERT.

Ingredients
65g (5 tbsp) unsalted butter, softened,
    plus extra for greasing
30ml (2 tbsp) clear blossom honey
120g (1 cup) icing sugar
100g (heaped $^3/_4$ cup) plain flour
30g (heaped $^1/_4$ cup) cocoa powder
1 egg white

Makes about 20

1 Preheat the oven to 180°C (350°). Line a large baking
sheet with baking parchment. Place the butter and honey
in a mixing bowl and beat using an electric hand mixer
until smooth and creamy.

2 Sift the sugar, flour and cocoa powder together then
gradually whisk into the creamed mixture. Mix well until
incorporated. At a low speed gradually add the egg whites.
When mixed in, increase the speed to high and whisk for 5
minutes until a smooth paste.

3 Spoon a tablespoon of the chocolate mixture on to the
prepared baking sheet. Using the back of a dessertspoon,
spread the mixture into a 8cm (3$^1/_4$in) diameter circle,
about 3mm ($^1/_8$in) thick. Repeat this process until the
baking sheet is covered in rounds or 'tuiles'. Bake for 4–5
minutes until slightly firm.

4 Leave to rest for 30 seconds. Remove the tuiles from the
baking sheet using a palette knife and when still warm,
drape each one over a lightly greased rolling pin and leave
until cool and crisp. Work quickly as the mixture will set
almost immediately. Alternatively, mould each tuile over
an inverted coffee mug or cup to make a chocolate basket.
If you need to, pop the tuiles back in the oven to soften
then resume shaping.

Chocolate chip cookies

THESE SERIOUSLY CHOCOLATEY COOKIES
SHOULD STILL BE SOFT AND GOOEY IN
THE CENTRE WHEN THEY COME OUT OF
THE OVEN.

Ingredients
110g (8 tbsp) unsalted butter, plus extra for greasing
50g (3$^1/_2$ tbsp) caster sugar
50g (3$^1/_2$ tbsp) soft brown sugar
1 free-range egg
$^1/_2$ tsp vanilla extract
150g (1$^1/_4$ cups) plain flour
$^1/_2$ tsp baking soda
175g (1 cup) semi-sweet or plain chocolate chips
20g (1$^1/_2$ tbsp) chopped walnuts (optional)

Makes about 20

1 Preheat the oven to 180°C (350°F) and lightly butter a
baking sheet or tray. Beat the butter and both types of
sugar together in a large mixing bowl until light and
creamy. Whisk in the egg and vanilla extract.

2 In a smaller bowl, sift the flour and baking soda together.
Gradually add this to the sugar and egg mixture and beat
until smooth. Fold in the chocolate chips and chopped
walnuts, if using.

3 Spoon a tablespoon (or teaspoon if making smaller
cookies) of the mixture at well-spaced intervals on to the
prepared baking sheet or tray. Bake for about 10 minutes
until golden. Leave to cool slightly then transfer to a wire
rack to cool.

Previous page: Chocolate tuiles
Opposite: Chocolate chip cookies

Whisky truffles

PERFECT WITH COFFEE FOLLOWING A MEAL, THESE BOOZY CHOCOLATE TRUFFLES ARE SO SIMPLE TO MAKE. YOU COULD ALSO USE YOUR FAVOURITE LIQUEUR INSTEAD OF WHISKY.

Ingredients
100ml (scant ½ cup) whipping cream
350g (12oz) plain chocolate, broken into pieces
100g (scant 1 cup) icing sugar, sifted
60ml (4 tbsp) whisky, warmed
100g (scant 1 cup) cocoa powder, for dusting

Makes about 20

1 Line a large baking tray with baking parchment. Bring the cream up to the boil in a saucepan then remove from the heat and stir in the chocolate pieces. Whisk until smooth, then whisk in the icing sugar.

2 Pour in the warm whisky and whisk again until smooth. Pour the mixture into a mixing bowl, cover with clingfilm and chill for about 6 hours until set.

3 When the mixture is set, dust a plate and your hands with cocoa powder. Divide the chocolate mixture into 20 equal portions – about the size of a walnut – and roll into balls in the palm of your hand. Roll the balls in the cocoa powder and leave to firm up in the fridge. Before serving, place the truffles in petit four cases.

Mocha swirls

THESE BITE-SIZED MORSELS LITERALLY MELT IN THE MOUTH AND HAVE A SLIGHT HINT OF COFFEE. THEY'RE GREAT WITH TEA, COFFEE, OR, OF COURSE, WITH OUR HOT CHOCOLATE, SEE PAGE 60.

Ingredients

60g (2oz) milk chocolate, broken into pieces
60g (2oz) plain chocolate, broken into pieces
200g (scant 1 cup) unsalted butter, softened
60g (4 tbsp) icing sugar, sifted
1 tbsp instant coffee granules
200g (1¾ cups) plain flour, sifted
60g (4 tbsp) cornflour, sifted

Makes 30 swirls

1 Preheat the oven to 180°C (350°F). Line a large baking tray with baking parchment.

2 Melt the milk and plain chocolate in a heatproof bowl placed over a saucepan of gently simmering water; stir gently until combined.

3 In a mixing bowl, whisk the butter and icing sugar together until light and pale.

4 Mix the coffee with 1 tablespoon boiling water and set aside. Add the melted chocolate to the butter and sugar mixture and stir until incorporated. Add the diluted coffee then fold in the flour and cornflour.

5 Spoon the mixture into a piping bag with a star nozzle and pipe 3cm (1¼in) rounds onto the prepared baking tray. Bake for 8–10 minutes – the biscuits should still be very soft. Remove from the oven and leave the swirls on the baking tray for 5–10 minutes then transfer to a wire rack to cool. The swirls can be stored in an airtight container for up to 5 days.

Dark chocolate fruit and nut

ADAPTED FROM THE BRITISH FAVOURITE CHOCOLATE FRUIT AND NUT BAR, THIS IS A RICHER ALTERNATIVE AND TRULY MELTS IN THE MOUTH.

1 Line a 26cm (10½in) x 31cm (12½in) x 2.5cm (1in) deep baking tray with baking parchment. Melt the chocolate and butter in a heatproof bowl placed over a saucepan of gently simmering water; stir until combined.

2 Fold the remaining ingredients into the chocolate and butter and mix until combined.

3 Spoon the mixture into the prepared tray and spread into an even layer, about 2cm (¾in) deep, using a spatula. Allow to set in the refrigerator for 4–5 hours. Remove from the tray and cut into bite-sized pieces.

Ingredients

200g (7oz) plain chocolate, broken into pieces
100g (scant ½ cup) unsalted butter, cubed
300g (11oz) condensed milk
150g (5½oz) gingernut biscuits, crushed
300g (1½ cups) dried apricots, chopped
200g (1¾ cups) pecan nuts, chopped
100g (scant 1 cup) macadamia nuts, chopped

Makes about 40

Coconut crunch

SMOOTH, CREAMY CHOCOLATE AND CRUNCHY COCONUT
GIVES THIS PETIT FOUR A TRUE TASTE OF PARADISE.

1 Line a 26cm (10½in) x 31cm (12½in) x
2.5cm (1in) deep baking tray with baking
parchment. Melt the chocolate and butter
together in a heatproof bowl placed over a
saucepan of gently simmering water then stir
until combined

2 Fold the remaining ingredients into the
chocolate and butter and mix until combined.

3 Spoon the mixture into the prepared tray
and spread into an even layer, about 2cm (¾in)
deep, using a spatula. Allow to set in the
refrigerator for 4–5 hours. Remove from the
tray and cut into squares.

Ingredients
200g (7oz) plain chocolate, broken into pieces
100g (scant ½ cup) unsalted butter, cubed
350g (12oz) condensed milk
250g (2½ cups) grated coconut, toasted
200g (scant 1 cup) dried glacé cherries, chopped

Makes about 20

Sauces and drinks

Vanilla and cinnamon hot chocolate

THIS IS A FABULOUS WINTER WARMER BUT TO BE HONEST, IT'S GREAT AT ANY TIME. YOU CAN ALWAYS ADD A SHOT OF YOUR FAVOURITE TIPPLE – BAILEY'S WORKS EXCEPTIONALLY WELL.

Ingredients
1 litre (4 cups) milk
$1/2$ vanilla pod, split and seeds scraped out
60g ($1/2$ cup) cocoa powder, plus extra for dusting
60g (4 tbsp) caster sugar
$1/4$ tsp cinnamon

To serve:
plain chocolate buttons
whipped cream

Serves 4

1 Carefully warm the milk and vanilla seeds in a saucepan, taking care not to let it boil. Remove the warm milk from the heat and whisk in the cocoa, sugar and cinnamon.

2 Place a few chocolate buttons in the bottom of 4 cups or paint melted chocolate inside the base of the glass. Pour in the hot chocolate. Spoon the whipped cream on top then dust with cocoa and serve.

Hot chocolate and sage drink

CHOCOLATE AND SAGE IS A FANTASTIC COMBINATION – YOU GET A SUBTLE KICK OF THE HERB AFTER THE INITIAL CHOCOLATE SENSATION.

Ingredients
1 litre (4 cups) full-cream milk
60g (4 tbsp) caster sugar
75g (5 tbsp) cocoa powder, plus extra for dusting
5 large fresh sage leaves, plus extra, to decorate (optional)

Serves 4

1 Carefully warm the milk with the sage leaves. Remove from the heat and allow to infuse for 1 hour. Pass the milk through a sieve and discard the sage leaves.

2 Return the milk to the saucepan with the sugar and cocoa powder and reheat, whisking well.

3 Whisk with a hand blender until frothy then pour into 4 heatproof glasses or mugs. Dust with cocoa and decorate with a sage leaf, if liked.

Previous page: Vanilla and cinnamon hot chocolate
Opposite: Hot chocolate and sage

Chocolate orange sauce

CHOCOLATE AND ORANGE ARE PERFECT
PARTNERS AS SHOWN IN THIS RICH,
AROMATIC SAUCE.

Ingredients
250ml (1 cup) milk
zest of 1 grated orange
200g (7oz) plain chocolate, broken into pieces

Makes 350ml (1¹/₂ cups)

Put the milk and orange zest in a saucepan and bring
up to the boil. Remove from the heat, add the
chocolate and whisk until melted.

Bitter chocolate sauce

THIS RICH, DARK CHOCOLATE SAUCE
WORKS SURPRISINGLY WELL WITH
ROASTED VENISON AND OTHER GAME.
BITTER CHOCOLATE IS THE PREFERRED
TYPE TO USE, AT LEAST 55–75 PER CENT
COCOA SOLIDS.

Ingredients
90ml (6 tbsp) red wine
2 shallots, finely chopped
600ml (2¹/₂ cups) fresh beef stock
25g (1oz) plain chocolate buttons

Makes about 200ml (scant 1 cup)

1 Heat the red wine in a saucepan with the chopped
shallots and cook briskly until the wine is reduced by
half. Pour in the beef stock and cook over a medium-
high heat until reduced by two-thirds.

2 Remove from the heat and pass through a fine sieve.
Add the chocolate buttons and whisk until melted.

White chocolate sauce

THIS IS AN EXTREMELY EASY SAUCE TO MAKE
AND LOOKS IMPRESSIVE POURED OVER DARK
CHOCOLATE ICE CREAM.

Ingredients
250ml (1 cup) milk
200g (7oz) white chocolate, broken into pieces

Makes about 350ml (1¹/₂ cups)

Bring the milk up to the boil in a saucepan. Pour the hot
milk over the chocolate and stir well until melted.

Dedication

To our dad Michael Tanner for the late night taxi service he provided picking us up from restaurants in the early days. Also for his perfectionism, dedication, passion and knowledge he gave us as children.

Acknowledgements

We would like to thank our sous chef Richard Farleigh, who helped in collating the recipes and testing. Naomi Osborne one of our pastry chefs who assisted in preparing the food for photography. All our staff at Tanners, especially Andrew "birchy" Birch for his infectious energy and humour!

A big thank you to speciality suppliers Forest Produce, who kindly provided the Callebaut chocolate we used in the recipes. Peter Cassidy for his superb photography, our agents at Limelight, Fiona Lindsay and Linda Shanks, and Jacqui Small for giving us the opportunity to write this book.

Finally, from James: a special thank you to Alex and the latest addition to the Tanner family, our baby daughter Megan. From Chris: a special thank you to my wife Steph for being there for me and a big kiss to my two little angels, Olivia and Isabelle

BAKING TERMS

UK	US
baking sheet	cookie sheet
baking tray	baking sheet
cake tin	cake pan
caster sugar	superfine sugar
chocolate, plain	semisweet or bittersweet (semisweet contains more sugar)
chocolate, white	white coating
double cream	heavy cream
flan tin	tart pan
full-cream milk	whole milk
greaseproof paper	waxed paper
icing sugar	confectioners' sugar
palette knife	spatula
plain flour	all-purpose flour
self-raising flour	self-rising flour
semi-skimmed milk	lowfat milk
single cream	light cream
springform tin	springform pan
vanilla pod	vanilla bean